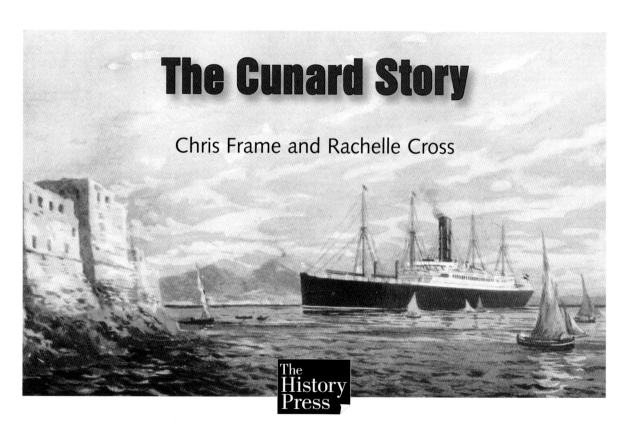

The Cunard Story

Chris Frame and Rachelle Cross

The
History
Press

Published in the United Kingdom in 2011 by
The History Press
The Mill · Brimscombe Port · Stroud · Gloucestershire · GL5 2QG

Reprinted 2015

British Library Cataloguing in Publication Data
A catalogue record for this book is available from the British
Library.

ISBN 978-0-7524-5914-1

Half title page: Carmania *was built to trial the turbine engine.* (Ian Boyle / Simplon Postcards)

Title page: *Cunard's* Saxonia *depicted in a postcard.* (Ian Boyle / Simplon Postcards)

➤ *The iconic* QE2 *meets the new* Queen Elizabeth *in Dubai, 2011.* (Cunard Line)

Typesetting and origination by The History Press
Printed in China

CONTENTS

ACKNOWLEDGEMENTS

We would like to thank everyone who helped us tell the Cunard story. We are extremely grateful to Ian Boyle for allowing us to use his superb collection of maritime photographs and postcards. His Simplon Postcard collection is viewable

➤ *The RMS* Queen Mary *departing Southampton.* (Colin Hargreaves)

online at www.simplonpc.co.uk and is one of the most extensive collections we've ever seen.

Special thanks to Bill Miller for writing the superb introduction for this book; Commodore R.W. Warwick for assisting us with historic Cunard imagery; Captain Ian McNaught for sharing with us his memories of *QE2*; Caroline Matheson from Cunard Line for sharing her thoughts of working with Cunard; John Langley of the Cunard Steamship Society for providing his thoughts about the Cunard Line; Colin Clarke from the Lancastria Association for helping clarify our queries regarding that ship; and Michael Pocock for allowing us access to his extensive collection of historic images, which can be seen online at www.maritimequest.com.

We are grateful as always to Michael Gallagher of the Cunard Line for assisting us with factual and photographic requests.

Thank you to the team at The History Press, especially Amy Rigg, Emily Locke, Glad Stockdale and Marc Williams for all their hard work on this book.

We are very grateful for the photographic assistance of Andrew Sassoli-Walker, Andy Fitzsimmons, Barry Brown, Britta Möller (Lloyd Werft), Colin Hargreaves, Edda Zacharias (Lloyd Werft), Frank Prudent, George Frame, George C. Griffiths, Janette Warner, John Hargreaves, Pam Massey, Paul A. Tenkotte PhD, Peter Williams, Ross Burnside, Russell Smith, Sam Warwick, Simon McGrath, Thad Constantine, William Brown and Wolfhard Scheer (Lloyd Werft).

INTRODUCTION

I've been madly in love with ocean liners since my earliest childhood, in the early 1950s. We were, in fact, all great 'friends', even neighbours. I lived close to the shore of the mighty Hudson River in New York. But I was on the 'other side', along the western shoreline of the river, in Hoboken, New Jersey. The great liners came and went, almost past my window, with great regularity. I saw the Cunarders all the time, sometimes as often as three or four times a week. The likes of the mighty *Queen Mary* and *Queen Elizabeth* were framed by the extraordinary Manhattan skyline – the soaring Empire State Building, for example, poking up above the top decks and twin funnels of, say, an outbound *Queen Elizabeth*. But I also remember many other occasions: the *Britannic* slipping off in a Friday afternoon rain, the inbound *Sylvania* on a frigid winter's morning, and the *Caronia* dressed in flags from end to end on a bright, sunlit summer's morning. It was all magic. There was nothing quite like Cunard, then and now. And ashore, at New York, they had the grandest, most impressive of all shipping offices along Lower Broadway's 'Steamship Row'. Cunard's headquarters was more a temple, with marble columns, art-filled ceilings, rows of mahogany desks and a complete company museum of superbly detailed models.

Today, Cunard is one of the oldest, most historic shipping lines still in business. The company was, in fact, saved and made much more profitable after being sold to Miami-based Carnival Corporation in 1998. As I write this, the 92,000-ton *Queen Elizabeth* is being fitted out in an Italian shipyard and being readied to join the

◄ *RMS* Queen Elizabeth. (Bill Miller Collection)

fleet in October 2010. Her fleet mates are the similar-sized *Queen Victoria* and the mighty 151,000-ton *Queen Mary 2*, which continues the tradition of Atlantic crossings. Happily, I too have written much about Cunard and its ships, including books of my own, and I am often a guest speaker for the Line's superb Enrichment Programme.

Cunard dates from 1840 and success, as well as popularity, was almost instant. Many of the company's ships were innovative and often ranked as the 'world's largest' and 'world's fastest'. Within seventy years, the then Liverpool-headquartered firm, the biggest and busiest on the North Atlantic, was capped by twin four-stackers, the immortal *Lusitania* and *Mauretania*. Even bigger, the exquisite *Aquitania* followed by 1914. Cunard pioneered in early cruising as well, running the very first full around-the-world cruise in 1922. But the 1930s peaked with the creation of the most famous and successful pair of Atlantic super liners ever, the brilliant *Queen Mary* and *Queen Elizabeth*. Later, during the Second World War, they were dubbed the most successful pair of troopships. Then, in 1948, Cunard added the splendid *Caronia*, the famed 'Green Goddess', the first big liner built for luxury cruising.

'Getting there is half the fun' was the most apt expression for Atlantic crossings, for which Cunard used no less than twelve liners in the 1950s. But the jet soon arrived and the age of ocean crossings was all but over; so the company, like others, turned more and more to lucrative, ever-expanding cruising. These days, you can cruise on a Cunarder from a three-night 'long weekend' trip to over 100 days around the world. And the grand tradition of fine service, food and entertainment continues – and perhaps in ways is even better than ever!

Hail to the great Cunard Line, its rich history and charismatic fleet, and to Chris Frame and Rachelle Cross for producing yet another fine book that reminds and enlightens us of that greatness. Three loud blasts to Cunard!

Bill Miller, 2010

The Cunard story started not in Great Britain or the United States, but in the Dominion of Canada. It was there, in Halifax, Nova Scotia, that Samuel Cunard was born in 1787.

Samuel Cunard was the son of master carpenter Abraham Cunard who, along with his wife Margaret, had migrated to Canada to work at the British garrison in Halifax. A loyalist, Abraham Cunard lived well in Halifax, becoming a wealthy landowner and timber merchant by the time of Samuel's birth.

Samuel Cunard was a brilliant child and developed a strong entrepreneurial spirit which would serve him well throughout his life. His business skills were evident by the time he reached seventeen, when he bought and managed his own general store in the city. He later joined his father in the family timber business and, using his skills, expanded into coal, iron, shipping and whaling.

During the war of 1812, Samuel Cunard volunteered for service in the 2nd Battalion of the Halifax Regiment of Militia. Here he rose to the rank of captain and gained a reputation with his troops as being a brilliant and fair-minded leader.

After his return from the war, he set about revolutionising the family business. During this time, Samuel Cunard held many public offices (including lighthouse commissioner) and maintained a reputation as not only a shrewd businessman but also an honest and generous citizen. Over time, his prominence and reputation in Halifax grew, and he became one of a group of twelve individuals who dominated the affairs of Nova Scotia.

Sir Samuel Cunard. (R.W. Warwick, *QE2: The Cunard Line Flagship Queen Elizabeth 2*)

Did you know?
Aboard *Britannia*, the fare to Halifax was 35 guineas, which included wines and spirits as well as food!

His interests became focused on both shipping and coal. His early investments in steam included co-founding a steam ferry company operating in Halifax Harbour (and later up the east coast of Canada). He was also involved in the pioneering steamship *Royal William*, which fed his enthusiasm for this new technology and its potential to move large vessels across the Atlantic.

It was therefore no surprise when Samuel Cunard relocated to Great Britain, in order to bid for the rights to run a British Government-subsidised transatlantic mail service between Great Britain and North America. Having won the contract, Samuel Cunard was granted a yearly subsidy and was able to formalise his business as the British & North American Royal Mail Steam Packet Co., which quickly became known (for simplicity's sake) as Cunard's Line.

Under the terms of the mail contract, Cunard Line was obliged to provide a fortnightly service using four steamships of similar size and speed. To this end, Samuel Cunard engaged the services of naval architect, Robert Napier, who was already well versed in steam technology.

The first of the Cunarders was RMS *Britannia*. She was a twin-paddle steam-powered vessel with a top speed of 9 knots, allowing her to make the transatlantic crossing in approximately fourteen days. She was joined by three near-sisters, *Acadia*, *Caledonia* and *Columbia*, over the

'Nothing smaller for sleeping in was ever made save coffins.'
Charles Dickens

Did you know?

Charles Dickens was an early passenger aboard *Britannia*. He described conditions as like being aboard 'a gigantic hearse with windows'.

following year, allowing Cunard to fulfil his Royal Mail obligations. Each of these ships wore the designation of Royal Mail Ship (RMS) due to their cargo.

While Cunard Line's ships were intended primarily to operate the mail service, Samuel Cunard's entrepreneurial mind saw the opportunity for him to increase his profits by carrying passengers aboard his ships. Space not dedicated to mail, cargo and machinery was provided to passengers, all of whom sailed in a single, spartan class of accommodation.

Life aboard the early Cunarders was far from comfortable. While considered superior to the slower, older sailing packets, a voyage by early steamship was by no means a pleasurable experience. Conditions were cramped and the food was far from

▲ *The first Cunarder, RMS* Britannia, *as depicted aboard the current flagship, QM2.* (Pam Massey)

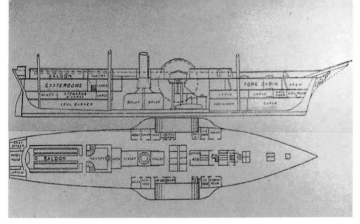

▲ *Deck plans of Cunard's first ship,* Britannia. (R.W. Warwick, *QE2: The Cunard Line Flagship Queen Elizabeth 2*)

gourmet. In fact, fresh food was provided by livestock carried aboard (refrigeration having not yet been installed aboard a ship). There was a cow for milk and chickens for eggs. One imagines that this must have resulted in a less than pleasant smell for those passengers unfortunate enough to be berthed near the animals.

Despite the lack of creature comforts, the fledgling Cunard Line flourished. Samuel

Cunard had selected the port of Boston as the American terminus of the new service, with a feeder run provided north to Halifax for Canadian passengers.

The selection of their port was a significant coup for Boston. So delighted were the citizens that Cunard had selected their port over rivals, such as New York, that when Samuel Cunard arrived in Boston aboard *Britannia* at the end of her maiden voyage, he was invited to no less than 1,873 dinner parties.

John Langley, Chairman of the Cunard Steamship Society, reflects on the significance of the Cunard service:

With the successful introduction of steam to the North Atlantic by Novascotian Samuel Cunard in 1840, transportation, communication and commerce between

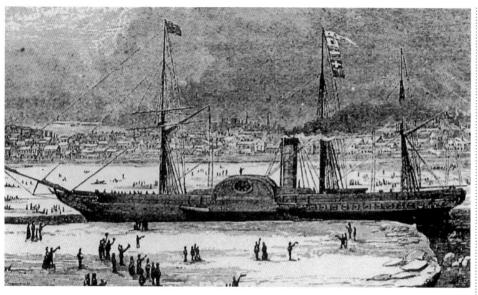

Did you know?

The Britannia (Boston) Cup was created in celebration of *Britannia*'s first arrival in Boston. It is now displayed aboard *Queen Mary 2*.

the Old and New Worlds was forever transformed. Henceforth, both the mails and passengers would cross the Atlantic according to schedule, as regular and dependable as land-based steam locomotives. Cunard's dream of creating an 'ocean railway' with his first quartet of steamships had become a reality.

▲ *Edward Knight Collins was one of Cunard's earliest rivals.* (R.W. Warwick, *QE2: The Cunard Line Flagship Queen Elizabeth 2*)

➤➤ *Collins Line's* Atlantic *was larger than its Cunard counterparts.* (R.W. Warwick, *QE2: The Cunard Line Flagship Queen Elizabeth 2*)

➤➤ Persia *at sea.* (R.W. Warwick, *QE2: The Cunard Line Flagship Queen Elizabeth 2*)

Cunard Line's popularity grew almost exponentially, especially in the port of Boston. The city held a strong sense of adoration for the company as well as Samuel Cunard himself.

This connection was particularly evident in the winter of 1844, when *Britannia* became trapped in ice at Boston Harbour. The late departure of *Britannia* would have seen her fail to maintain the scheduled mail service, resulting in hefty fines. However, the people of Boston, aware of *Britannia*'s plight, turned out en masse and, using pick axes and shovels, cut a channel through the ice allowing *Britannia* to escape.

For a brief period, Cunard enjoyed a near monopoly on the North Atlantic, being the only company offering regular scheduled crossings for both mail and passengers. It wasn't long, however, before other entrepreneurs and governments saw the success of Cunard Line and moved to stake their own claims on the lucrative transatlantic service.

In 1849, the American Postmaster General offered to subsidise an American company to establish their own transatlantic mail service, in order to reduce their reliance on the British.

Tenders were submitted and the first company to be awarded the American contract was the Collins Line, under the direction of Edward Knight Collins. Being in direct competition with Cunard, Collins had an ambitious plan to build five ships, each larger, faster and more luxurious than its Cunard counterpart. This saw the Collins Line not only secure its position as a dominant mail carrier, but also threaten the future of the Cunard passenger service.

Collins named his ships *Atlantic*, *Arctic*, *Adriatic*, *Baltic* and *Pacific*, and for a time they were extremely popular, cutting into Cunard's bottom line. In response to the American competition, Cunard introduced additional ships to its fleet, including the first iron-hulled paddle steamer, *Persia*. *Persia* proved to be faster than the Collins fleet, winning the speed record for the Atlantic crossing.

Despite the initial success, the Collins Line was plagued with a series of disasters which ultimately resulted in its demise. The disasters were largely attributed to the company policy of maintaining

➤ *Passage by steamship in the early years was dangerous.* (R.W. Warwick, *QE2: The Cunard Line Flagship Queen Elizabeth 2*)

Did you know?
During the Crimean War (1853–56) Cunard sent eleven ships to aid the war effort.

Did you know?
The term 'Blue Riband', to describe the westbound Atlantic speed record, was not widely used until 1910.

sailing schedules irrespective of weather conditions.

In contrast to the Collins Line policy, Samuel Cunard insisted that his captains maintain safety over speed, giving them a simple but poetic line of instructions: 'Your ship is loaded, take her; speed is nothing, follow your own road, deliver her safe, bring her back safe – safety is all that is required.'

The fall of the Collins Line was by no means the end of competition for Cunard. Both at home and abroad, new shipping companies were forming and an influx of larger and faster liners entered the transatlantic trade.

A notable competitor to Cunard was the British Oceanic Steam Navigation Co. Founded in 1868 by Thomas Henry Ismay, it is better known as the White Star Line, an identity it adopted after purchasing the name, house flag and goodwill of a defunct company.

Ismay set about creating his fleet through an exclusivity agreement with the Harland & Wolff shipbuilding company. This agreement precluded Cunard from having its ships built at the Northern Ireland shipyard. The first ship for the White Star transatlantic service was the *Oceanic*

(3,707 gross tons), which entered service in 1871. She was followed by five fleet mates of similar dimensions.

The White Star Line was not the only British competition for Cunard. In 1871 the Inman Line vessel, *City of Brussels*, eclipsed Cunard's *Scotia* as the fastest ship on the transatlantic service. That same year a new American competitor, the American Line, was founded as a branch of the Philadelphia Railroad Co.

In Europe, companies such as Norddeutscher Lloyd, Hamburg-Amerika Line and the Compagnie Générale Transatlantique (French Line) were beginning to gain popularity. The formation of the German Empire contributed significantly to the growth of the German lines, which would ultimately see them become a serious threat to Cunard.

Did you know?
Bathrooms made their first appearance at sea in 1870.

Did you know?
China (1862) was the first Cunarder to carry a significant number of steerage passengers.

· SAMUEL CUNARD ·

After founding the Cunard Line, Sir Samuel Cunard went on to see its growth to the premier shipping company on the North Atlantic.

He was married to Susan, daughter of William Duffus, on 4 February 1815. Together they had nine children.

In 1859 Cunard was created a Baronet by Queen Victoria for his services to the country. He was succeeded in Cunard Line and in the baronetcy by his son Sir Edward Cunard, 2nd Baronet.

Sir Samuel was the great-grandfather of Nancy Cunard.

He died at Kensington on 28 April 1865 and is buried there in Brompton Cemetery.

INNOVATIONS

With the competition on the Atlantic heating up, shipping lines had to rely on more than just the size of their ships to lure passengers. This led to a fierce one-upmanship as the various lines tried to outdo one another in terms of technology, luxury and style.

It was the Cunard *Bothnia*, in 1874, that introduced the first lounge for women, the first library at sea and the first system of electric bells used to call cabin attendants. *Bothnia* and her sister ship *Scythia* were also the first transatlantic liners to have a smoking room aboard. Prior to this, smokers were prohibited from smoking indoors.

In 1876, the British mail contracts expired, ending the previously negotiated subsidies. The new mail contracts were paid based on the weight of mail transported. Cunard now shared the mail service not only with the British Inman Line, which had held a contract since 1867, but also with German companies Norddeutscher Lloyd and Hamburg-Amerika. This, along with the effects of the Depression of 1873, resulted in Cunard Line having to reorganise themselves as a publicly listed company, the Cunard Steamship Co., in order to raise capital.

▼ *This colour postcard sought to emphasise Saxonia's bulk.* (Ian Boyle / Simplon Postcards)

Did you know?

Winston Churchill sailed aboard *Etruria* to America in 1895 and returned aboard the same ship in 1896.

The newly listed company commissioned the construction of four steel-hulled ships, the first of which entered service in 1881. *Servia* was the first Atlantic passenger ship to have electric lighting throughout, increasing not only safety standards but also passenger creature comforts.

In 1884, Cunard commissioned two new express liners, *Umbria* and *Etruria*, both of which were capable of achieving 19.5 knots and winning the Atlantic speed record. In addition to their speed, these ships were notable for being the first Atlantic liners to introduce refrigeration technology. This allowed for the removal of livestock, resulting in an increase in passenger space and an improvement of air quality aboard.

Umbria and *Etruria* made use of the screw propeller, each having a single propeller

"HANDS ACROSS THE SEA."

S.S. SAXONIA. (CUNARD LINE.) 14,280 TONS.

▲ Saxonia *in a period postcard symbolising 'hands across the sea' between the USA and UK.* (Ian Boyle / Simplon Postcards)

▲ Etruria, *and her sister Umbria, had a single-screw propeller and auxiliary sails.* (Michael Pocock / Maritime Quest)

▲▶ Lucania *was a new breed of Cunarder.* (Ian Boyle / Simplon Postcards)

located centrally at the stern of the ship. Despite their technological advances, the design of these ships included three large masts which could be fully rigged to provide auxiliary power. *Etruria* made use of her sails in 1902 when her single propeller shaft developed cracks whilst at sea. She was able to sail to a nearby ship, which took her in tow to the Azores for repairs.

White Star Line and Inman Line made their own advances, both introducing twin-screwed ships, which allowed them to surpass the Cunarders in speed and reliability by 1887.

Campania and *Lucania*, introduced in 1893, won back the speed record for Cunard. At 12,950 gross tons, these

Did you know?

Campania and *Lucania* (1893) could achieve the same top speed as Cunard's current *Queen Victoria* and *Queen Elizabeth*.

ships eclipsed all others in terms of size and offered the most luxurious first class accommodation afloat. With their twin-screw propellers, both ships were able to make the transatlantic crossing in less than six days.

Powered by triple expansion engines, these ships had the largest of this type of

CUNARD LINE.
S.S. "CAMPANIA"
HORSE POWER 30,000.
TONNAGE 12,950
LENGTH 620 FEET.

Did you know?
Immigrants in the late 1800s and early 1900s felt that the more funnels a ship had, the safer it was.

◄ Campania *at sea*.
(Ian Boyle / Simplon Postcards)

S. S. Campania, at Landing Stage, Liverpool

➤ Campania *as depicted on a period postcard.* (Ian Boyle / Simplon Postcards)

engine to be installed on a Cunard liner and represented the pinnacle of that technology. Generating 31,000ihp, the engines allowed these ships to achieve an average speed of 22 knots and a top speed of 23.5 knots. In 1901, *Lucania* was the first Cunard

R. M. S. LUCANIA.

ship to be fitted with wireless technology. *Campania*, *Umbria* and *Etruria* were also among the first equipped with wireless.

With the introduction of wireless aboard the Cunarders, new innovations were possible. The *Cunard Daily Bulletin*

➤ *A colour drawing of Campania from a period postcard.* (Ian Boyle / Simplon Postcards)

was the first daily newspaper offered aboard the fleet. It outlined Marconigram communication between the ship and other wireless stations, both on land and at sea. These daily updates helped to reduce the sense of isolation so often associated with those early transatlantic voyages.

Despite this impressive list of firsts, Cunard was not the only line making advances at this time. In Germany, Norddeutscher Lloyd launched *Kaiser Wilhelm der Grosse* in 1897. At over 14,000 gross tons and 655ft in length, she was easily the largest liner on the transatlantic trade.

She was the first liner built as a four-stacker, her large funnels further exaggerating her size. In 1898 she became the first German liner to win the speed record for the westbound transatlantic crossing, with a time of five days and twenty hours.

Although the first in this new class of super liner, she was not the only large four-stacker. The rival Hamburg-Amerika Line introduced its own flagship in 1900,

S.D. Kaiser Wilhelm II.

Deutschland, which was larger, faster and more luxurious than *Kaiser Wilhelm der Grosse*.

▲ Kaiser Wilhelm der Grosse *was the first of the four-funnel liners.* (Ian Boyle / Simplon Postcards)

.SS. "Albania"

➤ Albania *(7,640 gross registered tons) made her maiden voyage on 17 September 1901.* (Ian Boyle / Simplon Postcards)

Did you know?
The five-funnelled *Great Eastern* of 1858 became the first four-stacker when one of her funnels was removed.

In an effort not to be outdone by its rival, Norddeutscher Lloyd responded with *Kaiser Wilhelm II*, which at 25,530 gross tons and 706ft long was even larger than the *Deutschland*.

The commanding profiles of these ships, combined with the belief among the immigrant trade that their four funnels signified increased safety, resulted in these German ships being wildly successful.

Unable to match the size and speed of the new German liners, and unable to raise the funds to build vessels that could, Cunard set about investigating a new form of motive power for its ships. The Parsons Turbine had been invented in 1884 and had been mooted as a method of powering large ocean-going vessels.

Cunard in particular saw the potential of this technology; however, the economies of this engine were unknown. Cunard needed to understand whether the new technology would yield sufficient savings to warrant investing in the turbine. This was a significant undertaking as it meant not only investing in the physical machinery, but also in re-training their engineers, all of whom were experts in the existing reciprocating engine technology.

In order to test the Parsons Turbine against the reciprocating engine, Cunard built two ships of near-identical dimensions. *Caronia* was completed with the traditional reciprocating engines, while her sister *Carmania* was fitted with the Parsons Turbine.

▲ Carmania *proved that turbines were more economical than reciprocating engines.* (Ian Boyle / Simplon Postcards)

Did you know?

In 1899, *Carinthia* was taken over for the carriage of mules to South Africa for Boer War service.

CUNARD R.M.S. CARMANIA   TONNAGE 20,000

The two ships, each at over 19,500 gross tons, entered service in 1905 on the Liverpool–New York route. *Carmania* proved to be the more efficient of the two, able to achieve greater speeds with less fuel. Although she never matched the speeds achieved by the German liners, she did prove to be an important test case and, as a direct result, Cunard would favour turbine engines for over sixty years.

Despite their new technology, the continued success of the German four-stackers was of great concern to Cunard Line, which had no ships of similar class with which to challenge the German liners. The British Admiralty was also concerned by the advances of the Germans, in part due to issues of national pride, but more importantly due to the steadily building tension across Europe.

LANDING STAGE, LIVERPOOL

This situation was exacerbated by the sale of the White Star Line to American financier J.P. Morgan in 1902, following a failed attempt by him to purchase Cunard. This, coupled with the Inman Line having been absorbed into the American Line

German liners. In addition, with White Star Line now in American hands, the Admiralty had less direct control over the specifications of ships built for that line.

In the United States, J.P. Morgan had reorganised his shipbuilding interests to form the International Mercantile Marine Co. (IMM), absorbing the Dominion Line, Layland Line, American Line and Red Star Line. They were grouped along with White Star Line to form a formidable force on the North Atlantic.

The new group, under the direction of White Star Line's managing director, J. Bruce Ismay, set its sights on squeezing Cunard out of the market. This resulted in the British Admiralty entering into negotiations with Cunard and ultimately offering the company funding to build two large ships.

▲ Lusitania *won the Blue Riband for Great Britain.* (Michael Pocock / Maritime Quest)

several years before, resulted in Cunard being the only major British competitor left on the transatlantic service.

For the Admiralty, this was worrying as it meant that if war broke out, the British merchant navy would be unable to match the potential trooping capabilities of the

With the aid of a £2,600,000 Government loan, Cunard was able to build *Lusitania* and *Mauretania*, which became colloquially known as its 'Ocean Greyhounds'. Under the terms of the loan, the ships were to achieve a maximum speed of no less than 24 knots and be able to be converted into armed merchant cruisers should the need arise.

Q. T. S. S., Mauretania, (THE LARGEST VESSEL IN THE WORLD,) LEAVING THE TYNE.

S.S. MAURETANIA

To expedite their entry into service, the building contracts were awarded to two shipyards. *Lusitania* was built at the John Brown shipyard in Scotland, while *Mauretania* was constructed at Swan Hunter & Wigaham Richardson Ltd in England. While both ships were built from the same design, the shipyards were encouraged to compete to build a better ship. Due to this, there were noticeable differences between the two vessels, allowing them to be easily identified.

A common factor between the two ships was their narrow hull, a design requirement for their proposed use as armed merchant cruisers. The original design called for three stacks and the inclusion of reciprocating engines. However, following the success of the *Carmania* trials, both ships were fitted with the Parsons Turbine. To facilitate the use of the turbine engines and associated boilers, a fourth funnel was added.

During speed trials, the turbines caused significant vibration at high speeds. In response, the ships received strengthening beams and redesigned propellers before entering service, to reduce vibration.

CUNARD R.M.S. MAURETANIA   TONNAGE 31,000

◄ *This postcard of* Mauretania *aims to showcase her speed and size.* (Ian Boyle / Simplon Postcards)

FASTEST STEAMERS IN THE WORLD.

CUNARD LINE

As transatlantic passenger liners, *Mauretania* and *Lusitania* were highly successful, managing to capture the Blue Riband for the fastest westbound crossing. While *Lusitania* captured the speed record first (she entered service first), *Mauretania*

37030 Fishguard. R. M. S. Mauretania.

(known as coaling or bunkering) these vessels was an arduous and dirty task, which delayed the ships for days on each side of the Atlantic. Once the coaling process was complete, the ships had to be

▼ *An artist's rendition of Cunard's* Mauretania. (Ian Boyle / Simplon Postcards)

CUNARD LINE.

S.S. MAURETANIA *entering New York Harbor*

ultimately proved to be the faster of the two, holding the record from 1909 to 1929.

Although the two new Cunarders were able to make the transatlantic crossing in less than five days (*Mauretania*'s record was four days, ten hours and fifty-one minutes), they weren't able to achieve Cunard's long-held ambition of a two-ship weekly transatlantic service. Refuelling

➤ Mauretania *entered service after* Lusitania. (Ian Boyle / Simplon Postcards)

Did you know?

You could tell *Lusitania* and *Mauretania* apart by the shape of their air vents. *Lusitania*'s were shaped like low-laying oil barrels, while *Mauretania* had oversized white scoop-style vents.

R.M.S. MAURETANIA.

CUNARD LINE

washed down to remove coal dust from exterior areas, lengthening the turnaround process further. As a result, they required a third running mate in order to complete the weekly transatlantic service.

In December 1910, a running mate for *Lusitania* and *Mauretania* was laid down at the John Brown shipyard in Clydebank. This ship, which entered service on 30 May 1914, was the *Aquitania* and was fondly known as 'Ship Beautiful'.

While *Lusitania* and *Mauretania* were built for speed, *Aquitania* was designed to compete with the White Star Line's Olympic Class liners, which were renowned for their luxurious interiors. At over 45,000 gross tons each, *Olympic*, *Titanic* and *Britannic* were the world's largest liners and represented White Star Line's decision to concentrate on luxury over speed.

Aquitania was the pinnacle of pre-First World War passenger liners. The last of the four-stackers, she was significantly larger than her running mates and yet still appeared graceful. Her interiors were both comfortable and elegant. Even her second and third class passengers were treated to greater luxury than aboard her Olympic Class rivals.

First class amenities included a swimming bath, gymnasium and multiple promenade decks (both open and covered). The Louis XVI restaurant featured a double-height decorated ceiling, while the grill room was available for no extra tariff.

Less than two months after *Aquitania*'s maiden voyage, the First World War erupted. Being British-flagged ships, many Cunard vessels were called up for war service. Among those were the *Mauretania* and *Aquitania*, requisitioned on 4 August 1914 for use as armed merchant cruisers. *Lusitania* was also placed on the armed merchant cruiser list; however, she was never called into service.

Did you know?
Aquitania's second class passengers had their own gymnasium and Verandah Café, whilst third class passengers had a covered promenade deck!

➤ *Cunard's (then) largest ship,* Aquitania, *is launched.* (Ian Boyle / Simplon Postcards)

CUNARD LINER "AQUITANIA" LEAVING WAYS – ENTERING WATER

Although they received massive refits, *Mauretania* and *Aquitania* were found to be unsuitable for use as armed merchant cruisers and were returned to Cunard service. The outbreak of the war, however, had led to a significantly reduced demand

R. M. S. Aquitania (Cunard Line).
Length 902 ft. Breadth 97 ft.
Depth 92 ft. 6 inches.
Tonnage 47,000. Speed 23 knots.

Did you know?
Cunard completed building the Cunard Building in Liverpool in 1917. It forms part of Liverpool's 'Three Graces'.

for passage across the Atlantic Ocean and, as such, *Mauretania* was laid up at Liverpool.

On 7 May 1915 *Lusitania*, which had remained in passenger service on a reduced sailing schedule, was en route to

Cunard White Star   *Aquitania*

Liverpool via Queenstown (now Cobh) when she was struck by a German torpedo off the coast of Ireland and sunk, losing 1,198 lives. The sinking of the *Lusitania* contributed to the US decision to enter the First World War.

With the loss of *Lusitania*, *Mauretania* was required to re-enter passenger service on the North Atlantic run. Before this could happen, however, the ship was requisitioned by the Admiralty for use as a troopship in the Gallipoli campaign. The following month, *Aquitania* was also requisitioned for trooping duties, carrying soldiers to the Dardanelles. As troopships, both Cunarders were painted in a dazzle camouflage, designed to confuse enemy U-boats and ships.

Mauretania was converted to a hospital ship in August 1915, and placed into service to assist in the evacuation of the wounded from Gallipoli in October. After three voyages as a troopship, *Aquitania* was also converted to a hospital ship and

'… The torpedoing and sinking of the steamship *Lusitania* constitute a series of events which the of the United States has observed with growing concern, distress, and amazement.'
Extract from the first US Government Protest to the Imperial German Government

▼ *The waters around Great Britain became a war zone at the outbreak of the First World War.* (George Frame Collection)

OCEAN STEAMSHIPS.

CUNARD

EUROPE VIA LIVERPOOL
LUSITANIA

Fastest and Largest Steamer
now in Atlantic Service Sails
SATURDAY, MAY 1, 10 A. M.
Transylvania, Fri., May 7, 5 P.M.
Orduna, - - Tues.,May 18, 10 A.M.
Tuscania, - - Fri., May 21, 5 P.M.
LUSITANIA, Sat., May 29, 10 A.M.
Transylvania, Fri., June 4, 5 P.M.

Gibraltar–Genoa–Naples–Piraeus
S.S. Carpathia, Thur., May 13, Noon

NOTICE!

TRAVELLERS intending to
embark on the Atlantic voyage
are reminded that a state of
war exists between Germany
and her allies and Great Britain
and her allies; that the zone of
war includes the waters adja-
cent to the British Isles; that,
in accordance with formal notice given by the Imperial German Government, vessels flying
the flag of Great Britain, or of
any of her allies, are liable to
destruction in those waters and
that travellers sailing in the
war zone on ships of Great
Britain or her allies do so at
their own risk.

IMPERIAL GERMAN EMBASSY

WASHINGTON, D. C., APRIL 22, 1915.

HMHS AQUITANIA

◄ Lusitania's *sailing schedule above the
infamous notice from the Imperial German
Embassy.* (Michael Pocock / Maritime Quest)

▲ *Cunard's* Aquitania *as a hospital ship.*
(Ian Boyle / Simplon Postcards)

served in this role from December 1915 to January 1916. During this time, both ships were painted in the distinctive hospital ship colours of white hull and superstructure, with red crosses and green bands, to signify them as ships of peace.

In April 1916, the *Aquitania* was returned to Cunard and sent to the Harland & Wolff shipyard in Belfast for refurbishment. This refit was almost complete when, in November 1916, she was called up again by the Admiralty for further hospital duties.

Mauretania spent the remainder of 1916 carrying Canadian troops to France, and both ships spent 1917 laid up, *Aquitania* on the Solent and *Mauretania* on the Clyde. In 1918, both liners transported American troops to Europe, *Mauretania* alone carrying over 30,000 American troops.

At the end of hostilities, *Mauretania* and *Aquitania* were used to repatriate American and Canadian troops. By the end of 1919, both ships had been returned to Cunard and given refurbishments before returning to passenger service.

Due to the loss of *Lusitania* during the war, Cunard could no longer maintain their three-ship transatlantic service. However,

◀ *The heroic* Carpathia *was sunk during the First World War.* (Michael Pocock / Maritime Quest)

Did you know?
Cunard's *Carpathia* was the only ship to rescue passengers from *Titanic*. *Carpathia* was later sunk on the Atlantic in July 1918 after being hit by three torpedoes.

Did you know?
Berengaria was named after Queen Berengaria, wife of Richard the Lionheart.

help came in the way of war reparations. The British were awarded the Hamburg-Amerika liners *Imperator* and *Bismarck*. A joint agreement between Cunard and the White Star Line saw *Imperator* sail under Cunard management, while *Bismarck* (still under construction) was completed as *Majestic* for the White Star Line.

Imperator was refurbished and entered service under her German name in March 1920. She did not remain in service with this name for long, and after a major overhaul was renamed *Berengaria*, becoming the flagship of the Cunard fleet.

Despite being compensated for the use of its ships and provided with war reparations for ships lost, the cost of war was high for Cunard. In total, twenty-two Cunard ships were lost in the First World War, as well as many crew, including experienced captains.

> ## · CUNARD WAR MEMORIAL ·
>
> Outside the Cunard Building in Liverpool stands the Cunard War Memorial. Unveiled in 1921 by the Earl of Derby, and designed by architect Arthur Davis, it is dedicated to those Cunard employees lost during the First World War and later the Second World War.

In the years that followed the First World War, Cunard set about rebuilding its devastated fleet. Fortunately for the line, with the introduction of *Berengaria* they were able to re-establish the three-ship weekly transatlantic service relatively quickly.

Cunard's pre-war competitors were facing a very different prospect. The German lines, having lost their larger ships both

FASTEST OCEAN SERVICE IN THE WORLD

CUNARD

SOUTHAMPTON, CHERBOURG AND NEW YORK

R.M.S. "MAURETANIA"   R.M.S. "BERENGARIA"   R.M.S. "AQUITANIA"

◄ *Cunard's premier liners,* Mauretania, Berengaria *and* Aquitania. (Ian Boyle / Simplon Postcards)

➤ Mauretania *in Cruising White.* (Bill Miller Collection)

through military action and also reparations, were no immediate threat to Cunard Line.

Another of Cunard's major competitors, the White Star Line, was struggling to establish its own three-ship weekly service.

CUNARD LINE   R M S. "BERENGARIA"   TONNAGE 52,300

◄ *Cunard's new flagship* Berengaria, *the former* Imperator. (Ian Boyle / Simplon Postcards)

CUNARD R.M.S. AQUITANIA   TONNAGE 45,650

Having lost *Titanic* in 1912, and *Britannic* to a mine during the war, *Olympic* was the only large ship available to them immediately following the Armistice.

White Star Line had to wait until 1922 before *Majestic* (formerly *Bismarck*) was completed and ready to enter service. She was paired with *Olympic* on the transatlantic run, with a third ship, *Homeric* (formerly the Norddeutscher Lloyd liner SS *Columbus*), entering service that same year.

The White Star Line found its weekly service difficult to maintain. Although *Homeric* did gain a popular following on the transatlantic run, her top speed of 18.5 knots meant that she was far slower than her fleet mates. While the Cunard trio, along with *Olympic* and *Majestic*, had been converted to burn oil shortly after the war, *Homeric* remained coal powered until

Did you know?
The 'A-Class' liners were so named because all of them had names starting with the letter A.

◄ Aquitania *against the New York skyline.* (Ian Boyle / Simplon Postcards)

➤*Berengaria became
Cunard's flagship.*
(Ian Boyle / Simplon
Postcards)

1924. This, coupled with her slower speed, resulted in White Star's schedules being less reliable than Cunard's.

Building on their success, Cunard introduced a number of new liners in the early 1920s, including the 'A-Class' ships. These intermediate-sized liners (approx. 14,000 gross tons each) were used on a number of routes between Europe and North America.

In 1922 Cunard Line pioneered the world cruise, sending its ship *Laconia* on a four-month circumnavigation of the globe. The voyage called at twenty-two ports and was so successful that future world voyages were planned.

When the stock market crashed in 1929, Cunard was once again facing serious competition from the German lines. The Norddeutscher Lloyd liners, *Bremen* and *Europa*, had eclipsed the Cunarders in size,

CUNARD R.M.S. BERENGARIA   TONNAGE 52,700

Cunard R.M.S. Mauretania

TONNAGE 31,000

speed and luxury. *Bremen* was renowned as the world's fastest liner, taking the Blue Riband from *Mauretania*. Paired with *Europa*, these ships were the first capable of achieving over 27 knots and operated an express transatlantic service.

1199 C. R. Hoffmann
Southampton.

R.M.S. "BERENGARIA."
BALLROOM.

52,226 Tons

The introduction of these two large German liners inaugurated a new era of competition between Europe's major shipping lines. *Bremen*'s reign as the fastest liner was short-lived, being eclipsed in 1931 by the Italia Line's *Rex*. *Rex* was paired with

1162. C. R. Hoffmann.
Southampton.

R.M.S "BERENGARIA."
First Class Smoking Room.

52,226 Tons

a near sister, the *Conte di Savoia*, which, although slightly slower, was the first liner to include stabiliser technology.

The advance of the European shipping lines on the transatlantic run was of deep concern to both Cunard and the British

1003 C. R. Hoffmann
Southampton

R.M.S. MAURETANIA. 31,000 Tons.
Length 760 ft.   Breadth 87 ft. 6 ins.

◄ Mauretania *was far smaller than her fleet mates.* (Ian Boyle / Simplon Postcards)

Admiralty. Cunard's ageing trio, *Mauretania*, *Berengaria* and *Aquitania*, were losing their ability to capture the passenger trade, while the Government was all too aware of the militarisation potential for the German and Italian liners, should war break out again.

Cunard responded by laying down an 80,000-ton ship, known as 'Hull 534', at the John Brown shipyard in Scotland on 1 December 1930. Across the Channel in France, the French Line laid down the *Normandie* on 26 January 1931. At over 79,000 tons, *Normandie* was intended to rival Cunard's 'Hull 534', while also eclipsing all other ships in opulence and style.

In December 1931, construction was halted on 'Hull 534' due to financial hardship caused by the Great Depression. The shipyard's workforce was laid off, devastating the community of Clydebank which relied heavily on the shipyard for employment.

The incomplete hull of 534 lay on the slipway rusting for more than two years. Imagery of the huge rusting hulk became synonymous with the effect of the Great Depression in Britain.

In France, the French Government had stepped in, providing funds to ensure the completion of *Normandie*. *Normandie* was held up as a symbol of the strength of France and their ability to weather the financial storm. On 29 October 1932, three years to the day since the stock market crash, *Normandie* was launched, witnessed by over 200,000 spectators.

The White Star Line, once again a British shipping company (having been purchased in 1927 by the Royal Mail Steam Packet Co.), was facing its own difficulties. Construction of its new 300m-long super liner, to be called *Oceanic*, had been cancelled, with work ceasing on 23 July 1929. In 1930, White Star Line, for the first time in sixty-one years, declared a

◄ Mauretania *and* Olympic *laid up awaiting scrap.* (Michael Pocock / Maritime Quest)

loss, with a bank overdraft of £1,239,382. Despite this loss, work continued on two smaller ships, *Britannic* and *Georgic*.

The British Government, concerned by the continued decline of British superiority on the transatlantic, received calls for assistance from both Cunard and White Star. A report was commissioned by Clydebank MP David Kirkwood, which found that it was in the nation's best interest to complete 'Hull 534', creating much-needed jobs in the region.

In response to the report and the shipping companies' pleas for help, the Government agreed to provide loans and subsidies to allow the completion of 'Hull 534', as well as a sister ship, under the proviso that the two lines merged. Negotiations began in 1933, and by April 1934 work had recommenced on 'Hull 534'. The companies officially merged on 10 May 1934, to form Cunard-White Star, with Cunard maintaining the controlling interest.

Did you know?
MV *Britannic* and MV *Georgic*, the last liners to be built by White Star prior to the merger, remained in their White Star livery for their entire service life.

As work neared completion on 'Hull 534', a launch date of 26 September 1934 was set. The ship was christened *Queen Mary* by HM Queen Mary, in the presence of King George V and approximately 250,000 spectators. RMS *Queen Mary* was moved to the fitting-out basin for work to continue.

C. R. Hoffmann, Southampton.
1260

CUNARD WHITE STAR LINER "QUEEN MARY."
THE WORLD'S LARGEST LINER AND HOLDER OF THE BLUE RIBAND.
LENGTH 1,020 FT. HEIGHT FROM MAST-HEAD TO WATER-LINE 200 FT. FROM TOP OF FIRST FUNNEL TO WATER-LINE 146 FT. TONNAGE 80,773.
SPEED EXCEEDING 30 KNOTS. THE LARGEST AND FASTEST SHIP IN THE WORLD. ACCOMMODATION FOR 5,000 PASSENGERS.
LAUNCHED AT CLYDEBANK BY HER MAJESTY QUEEN MARY, 26TH SEPTEMBER, 1934.

◄ *Queen Mary was the pride of the British merchant fleet.* (Ian Boyle / Simplon Postcards)

In France, the French Line flagship *Normandie* was readied for passenger service. On 29 May 1935, she departed on her maiden voyage. A very fast ship, *Normandie* was able to capture the Blue Riband for France, taking the honour from Italy's *Rex*.

By 1936, *Queen Mary*'s interior was nearing completion. Unlike *Normandie*, whose interiors were opulent and over-stated (*Normandie*'s Grand Saloon, for

➤ Queen Mary *held the speed record until 1952.* (Ian Boyle / Simplon Postcards)

1266 C. R. Hoffmann, Southampton.

CUNARD WHITE STAR LINER "QUEEN MARY."
The World's Largest and Fastest Liner.
CABIN CHILDRENS' PLAYROOM

80,773 Tons.

◄ *Queen Mary had a children's room, much to the delight of travelling families.* (Ian Boyle / Simplon Postcards)

example, was based on the Hall of Mirrors in Versailles), Cunard-White Star opted for a more understated elegance aboard their new flagship. The ship was finished in an Art Deco style, a vast departure from the Edwardian era interiors of *Aquitania* and

Mauretania. Queen Mary's interiors were comfortable rather than opulent, resulting in her ultimately becoming a far more popular ship than her French rival.

A sister ship for *Queen Mary* was announced in February 1936. The new ship was to be slightly larger than her sister, and was built at the same shipyard.

➤ Queen Mary's *interior was quite different from past Cunard ships.* (Ian Boyle / Simplon Postcards)

1268 C. R. Hoffmann, Southampton.

CUNARD WHITE STAR LINER "QUEEN MARY."
The World's Largest and Fastest Liner
MAIN CABIN SHOPPING CENTRE.

80,773 Tons

She was given the building designation of 'Hull 552'.

On 27 May 1936, *Queen Mary* set sail on her maiden voyage. Before departing on this voyage, King George V and Queen Mary toured the ship. It had been hoped that the ship would capture the Blue Riband on her first crossing; however, she was delayed by fog.

Queen Mary first captured the Blue Riband in August 1936. She held it for a year, until the *Normandie* made her best-ever crossing in 1937, recapturing the award for France. A year later, the *Queen Mary* made the crossing in three days, twenty-one hours and forty-eight minutes. This time she held the record until 1952!

Construction on 'Hull 552' commenced on 4 December 1936. She was launched on 27 September 1938 by HM Queen Elizabeth (later the Queen Mother), whom the ship was also named after. It had been intended for King George VI to attend the launch; however, due to the worsening political situation in Europe, he was unable to. The Queen used this opportunity to relay a message of peace and goodwill.

RMS *Queen Elizabeth* was moved to the fitting-out basin and work progressed on completing the liner. Her exterior boasted a far more modern appearance than that of *Queen Mary*. The years between finalising *Queen Mary*'s design and starting work

'Toured the new *Queen Mary* today.
Not as bad as I expected.'
HM Queen Mary

▲ Queen Elizabeth *entered service as a troopship.* (Michael Pocock / Maritime Quest)

open decks. In fact, she was often compared to the much smaller second *Mauretania*, which was launched several months prior to the Queen at Cammell Laird shipyard in Birkenhead, England – both ships sported the same general appearance when viewed from a distance.

War broke out in September 1939 with the German invasion of Poland. For the second time in the twentieth century, the Cunard-White Star fleet was in danger of attack. While the *Queen Mary* was safe in New York, having just completed her 143rd crossing, *Queen Elizabeth* was unable to leave Clydebank due to the tidal movements of the River Clyde.

on *Queen Elizabeth* allowed for more modern machinery, including fewer boilers, resulting in the new Queen sporting two funnels, rather than three.

Queen Elizabeth's superstructure further benefited from modern ventilation technology, similar to that used on *Normandie*, which gave her clutter-free

'The stateliest ship now in being.'
King George V speaking of RMS *Queen Mary*

We proclaim our belief that by the grace of god and by man's patience and goodwill, order may yet be brought out of confusion and peace out of turmoil. With that hope and prayer in our hearts we send forth upon her mission, this noble ship.

HM Queen Elizabeth

On 26 February 1940, having finally made the short journey to the Tail O' The Bank, the ship, painted entirely in grey and with a degaussing coil added, anchored to await further instructions. The following day the ship, yet to have her sea trials, was handed over to Cunard-White Star.

While the public believed that the *Queen Elizabeth* would make her way to Southampton, where a fitting-out berth was waiting for her, the crew were informed that Winston Churchill had ordered the ship to leave British waters, as it was a priority target for the Luftwaffe. No destination was set and the crew, who had previously signed articles for the trip to Southampton, were given new contracts for a voyage to international waters. Members of the crew who were unwilling to sign new articles were disembarked and detained until the ship sailed.

On 2 March 1940, the King's messenger arrived with sealed orders which were only to be opened once the ship was at sea. *Queen Elizabeth* sailed that day at 7.30a.m. The ship headed towards Northern Ireland. At eleven o'clock that evening, Captain Townley opened the sealed orders to reveal his destination: New York.

The untried ship, still with her launching gear attached, made a dash across the

Did you know?
Southampton was bombed by the Luftwaffe at the same time as *Queen Elizabeth* was expected to arrive in the port.

Atlantic towards safety at a speed of 27½ knots. Six days later, the ship arrived in New York and was berthed alongside *Mauretania*, *Normandie* and *Queen Mary*.

The Queens were not to be together for long. *Queen Mary* departed for Sydney on 21 March. There she would be converted to a troopship at the Cockatoo drydock on Cockatoo Island, before joining the veteran *Aquitania* on trooping duties to the Gulf of Suez.

Mauretania had left New York the previous day, also bound for Sydney. While *Queen Mary* would make the voyage

➤ Queen Mary *in her wartime colours.* (Ian Boyle / Simplon Postcards)

I send you my heartfelt congratulations on the safe arrival in New York of the *Queen Elizabeth*. Ever since I launched her in the fateful days of 1938 I have watched her progress with interest and admiration. Please convey to Captain Townley my compliments on the safe conclusion of her hazardous maiden voyage.

Queen Elizabeth on hearing of RMS *Queen Elizabeth*'s safe arrival in New York

via Trinidad, Cape Town and Fremantle, *Mauretania* was routed via Panama, San Francisco and the Pacific islands of Hawaii

in an effort to minimise the risk of losing both ships to the enemy.

Queen Elizabeth sailed for Singapore on 13 November 1940, where she was converted into the world's largest troopship. In April 1941, she rendezvoused with *Queen Mary* in Sydney. Both ships joined *Aquitania* and *Mauretania*, as well as the *Nieuw Amsterdam* and *Ile De France* on the troop transportation run.

On 17 June 1940, Cunard-White Star's *Lancastria* was sunk off Saint-Nazaire whilst taking part in Operation Ariel. So appalling was the loss of life, that the British

◄ *Mauretania was used for trooping duties.* (George Frame Collection)

Government banned public announcement of the disaster. As a result of this ban, it was first reported in the *New York Times*.

The two remaining White Star liners, *Britannic* and *Georgic*, did not escape war service. Both ships were called up

CUNARD LINE   R.M.S "LANCASTRIA"   GROSS TONNAGE 16,300

➤ Lancastria *was sunk with a shocking loss of life.* (Ian Boyle / Simplon Postcards)

for trooping duties. The *Britannic* carried approximately 180,000 troops during the course of the war, travelling a total of 326,673 nautical miles.

Georgic was not so lucky. On 14 July 1941, whilst anchored at Port Tewfik, Suez, the ship was bombed by the Luftwaffe shortly after midnight. Two bombs created considerable damage, above and below the water line, causing the oil and ammunition to catch fire. Although the ship was severely damaged, the captain ordered the ship moved so as not to block the channel. *Georgic* was driven on to a reef in the middle of Suez Bay, where she was left

'Splendid! Very good indeed. I never had any doubts about her getting over.'
Winston Churchill on hearing of RMS *Queen Elizabeth*'s safe arrival in New York

Did you know?

Legend has it that Cunard-White Star intended to name 'Hull 534' *Queen Victoria*, in keeping with company tradition of giving its ships names ending in 'ia'. However, when the Chairman of the Cunard-White Star Line asked the King's permission to name the ocean liner after 'Britain's greatest Queen', King George V said his wife would be delighted. Thus the ship was named *Queen Mary*.

to burn out. She was later refloated and returned to Harland & Wolff, where she was given an extensive refit and eventually returned to service.

On 7 December 1941, the United States entered the war after the Japanese attack on Pearl Harbour. At this time, *Queen Mary* was on the Clyde and *Queen Elizabeth*

was in Sydney. Seven weeks after America entered the war, *Queen Elizabeth* was sent to Canada for dry docking. *Queen Mary* remained on the Clyde, and both ships were briefly kept in the relative safety of their respective ports due to the high number of German and Japanese U-boats in operation. By 1942, however, both Queens were being used to transport American servicemen to Europe, having been converted to carry over 15,000 troops each per voyage.

◄ Cunard-White Star's *Georgic was bombed by the Luftwaffe.* (George Frame Collection)

➤ *Escorts were sent to protect the troopships.* (George Frame Collection)

On 12 September 1942, Cunard-White Star's *Laconia* was torpedoed and sunk by German U-boat U-156. At the time, *Laconia* was carrying soldiers and civilians, as well as Italian prisoners of war.

U-156's captain, Kapitänleutnant Werner

Hartenstein, and his crew, immediately commenced rescue operations and headed to rendezvous with Vichy French ships under the Red Cross banner. En route, the U-boats were attacked by a US Army B-24 Liberator bomber.

This event forever changed the operations of the German U-boat fleet, which

◄*The two Queens,* Mary *and* Elizabeth, *ending their wartime service.* (Ian Boyle / Simplon Postcards)

abandoned the practice of attempting to rescue civilian survivors under the 'Laconia Order'. It set the precedent for the subsequent unrestricted submarine warfare, not only within the German navy, but also for the United States navy.

Less than a month after the sinking of *Laconia*, *Queen Mary* was involved in the sinking of another British ship. On 2 October 1942, *Queen Mary* was approaching the Irish coast en route to Scotland. Her escort was the light cruiser HMS *Curacoa*, which crossed the path of the oncoming *Queen Mary*, resulting in the Cunarder slicing the smaller cruiser in half. Under strict orders not to stop for any reason, *Queen Mary*

Did you know?

Winston Churchill made four wartime crossings aboard *Queen Mary*.

was forced to continue on; however, four other destroyer escorts were able to rescue survivors from the ocean.

Queen Mary and *Queen Elizabeth* continued their trooping duties for the remainder of the war years. Both ships carried between 10,000 and 15,000 troops on each voyage. *Queen Mary*, to this day, holds the record for the most people carried on a single crossing, 16,082.

At the end of the war, the Cunarders, including *Queen Elizabeth*, *Queen Mary*, *Mauretania* and *Aquitania*, saw further service, repatriating Allied soldiers. *Mauretania* undertook the first relocation of Canadian war brides in February 1946, with both Queens, as well as *Aquitania* and *Britannic*, participating in the massive relocation effort.

On 6 March 1946, it was announced that *Queen Elizabeth* would be the first passenger liner to be released from Government service. She was returned to Clydebank, where she was finally converted into the world's largest passenger liner. Despite six years of wartime service, she was given her full builder's trials and sea trials before being officially accepted by Cunard-White Star.

Queen Mary's demobilisation occurred on 27 September 1946, with a ten-month refurbishment required to bring the ship back to her pre-war glory. *Mauretania* returned to passenger service in 1947. Other ships, such as the veteran *Aquitania*, would not see passenger service again. The

▼ Queen Elizabeth: *then the world's largest liner.* (Ian Boyle / Simplon Postcards)

ship, which had survived both world wars, required too much refurbishment to be economically viable, and left Southampton for the final time in 1950, bound for the scrapyard.

In 1947, Cunard purchased the remaining White Star holding in the company, and dropped the White Star name and flag. That same year, the company finally realised its long-held dream of running a two-ship

➤ Queen Mary *is still one of the most beloved ships of all time.* (Ian Boyle / Simplon Postcards)

weekly transatlantic service with *Queen Elizabeth* and *Queen Mary*. The ships were joined on the transatlantic run by the refurbished *Mauretania* and *Britannic*, while Cunard set about rebuilding its lost fleet.

Plans were finalised for Cunard's first purpose-built cruise ship, the dual-purpose *Caronia*. Initially intended to be a running mate for *Mauretania*, *Caronia* entered service in 1949 painted in four shades of green. Nicknamed the 'Green Goddess', she included such features as air conditioning and an outdoor swimming pool, and would pioneer cruising voyages around the world as well as complete irregular transatlantic crossings.

Georgic, despite her Second World War refloating and refurbishment, was no longer able to be used as a premier

Did you know?
Caronia had the largest funnel of any Cunarder, weighing 125 tons. It measured 16.15m wide, had a breadth of 8.07m and a height of 14.02m.

▲ *A rare colour image of* Queen Elizabeth *from the air.* (Ian Boyle / Simplon Postcards)

R.M.S. "CARONIA." CUNARD WHITE STAR LINE

▲ Queen Mary, *a beloved Cunarder.* (Ian Boyle / Simplon Postcards)

▲► *Cunard's cruise ship,* Caronia, *had a loyal following.* (Ian Boyle / Simplon Postcards)

transatlantic liner. The ship, now with only a single mast and funnel, suffered from constant vibration, making for a less than pleasant voyage. As a result, she was used for the immigrant service to Australia and New Zealand.

The early 1950s were considered to be a golden age for Cunard. *Queen Elizabeth* and *Queen Mary* ran the premier transatlantic service with far less competition than pre-war Cunard had seen. *Caronia's*

cruising itineraries had proved very popular, with guests booking out suites aboard for months at a time, while the smaller combination cargo/first class liners *Media* and *Parthia* were becoming popular with celebrities, who appreciated their luxury and privacy.

In 1952, *Queen Mary* lost her crown as the fastest ocean liner on the North Atlantic. The American SS *United States* had been built with the assistance of the

Cunard White Star *Media*

US Government, who had seen the value of the *Queen Elizabeth* and *Queen Mary* as troopships during the Second World War. The SS *United States* was rumoured to have topped 46 knots during her sea trials, and captured the Blue Riband on her maiden voyage.

Despite losing the speed record, *Queen Mary* and her sister *Queen Elizabeth* maintained their popularity, with sufficient demand on the North Atlantic to support all of the large transatlantic liners. The Cunard experience was much beloved, and this was reflected in the company's marketing slogan of 'Getting there is half the fun!'

During 1952, Cunard tested the first fin stabilisers aboard the *Media*. The trials were successful, resulting in stabilisers being added to all Cunard ships.

In 1954, the Cunard fleet was bolstered by the addition of the four Saxonia Sisters. These ships, *Saxonia*, *Ivernia*, *Carinthia*

◀▲ *Her cruising role took* Caronia *to exotic destinations.* (Ian Boyle / Simplon Postcards)

▲ Media *was popular with celebrities due to her intimate nature.* (Ian Boyle / Simplon Postcards)

79

Cunard R.M.S. Parthia

and *Sylvania*, operated a service between Liverpool and the Canadian ports of Montreal and Quebec.

The good times were not to last. The introduction of regular jet services was the beginning of the end for the transatlantic

S.S. SAXONIA, *CUNARD LINE*
21,637 GROSS TONS   LENGTH 608 FT.   BEAM 80 FT.   SPEED 20 KNOTS.

◄ *An artist's impression of the new* Saxonia. (Ian Boyle / Simplon Postcards)

liner. In 1957, for the first time, more passengers crossed the Atlantic by air than by sea.

With a decrease in passengers, Cunard, along with its competitors, began to retire old tonnage and investigate new methods

Cunard "Carmania"

to help make ends meet. *Britannic* made the final departure of a White Star-built ship from Liverpool in 1960, when she left for the ship breakers (*Georgic* having been scrapped in 1956).

Media and *Parthia* left the fleet in 1961, having been sold to other shipping lines.

Media became the Italian immigrant ship *Flavia*, while *Parthia* was used in the Pacific by her new British owners.

That same year, Cunard shelved plans for a new liner, code-named Q3. This ship was intended to be a three-class liner of similar dimensions to the existing Queens and would have been a replacement for *Queen Mary*. However, her three-class design and large dimensions made her impractical in the age of the jet.

In 1962, Cunard formed a joint venture with the British Overseas Airways Corporation (BOAC) to form BOAC-Cunard, a small subsidiary airline that operated flights to North America and the tropics.

That same year, Cunard sent *Mauretania* cruising, having her painted in the same green livery as *Caronia*. The year 1962 also

◄ *There is no sight more impressive than a Queen at sea.* (Ian Boyle / Simplon Postcards)

saw changes made to the Saxonia Sisters, with *Saxonia* and *Ivernia* being refurbished for cruising. Their aft decks were altered to include an outdoor lido area, as well as a swimming pool, and they were renamed *Carmania* and *Franconia* respectively. They cruised the Caribbean and Mediterranean during the winter, while operating on the transatlantic during peak summer seasons.

Carinthia and *Sylvania* were also sent cruising after being given their own refurbishments. These refits, far less extensive than those afforded to *Carmania* and *Franconia*, were insufficient to attract a high number of cruising passengers, making the ships far less successful in this role than their fleet mates.

Even the great Queens, now operating virtually empty on the transatlantic run, were sent cruising to help make ends meet. *Queen Elizabeth* was given a cruising refit, with air conditioning installed throughout the ship and an aft lido area, including swimming pool, added. However, Cunard's converted ocean liners were not successful as cruise ships. The Queens were simply too large, with drafts too deep to enter cruising ports in the Caribbean and Mediterranean.

Did you know?
Cunard tried to enter the airline business more than once, running joint ventures with BOAC and Eagle Airways.

The realisation that the current fleet was unsuitable for cruising resulted in the design of a new dual-purpose liner code-named Q4. At 293m long and with a draft of 9.9m, she would be small enough to transit the Panama Canal and shallow enough to be suitable as a cruise ship.

Cunard applied to the British Government for a loan of £17.6 million to build Q4. Tenders for the construction of this new liner were received in 1964, with the contract being awarded to John Brown on 30 December of that year. She was given the building number of 736. Despite the Government loan, Cunard had to mortgage eleven ships, including passenger ships and vessels from its cargo operations, in order to complete the new ship.

In July 1965, the keel plates of Number 736 were laid. That September, *Mauretania* completed her final Cunard voyage, a Mediterranean cruise. Continued losses meant that she was unsustainable in her cruising role.

In 1966, BOAC bought out Cunard's share in BOAC-Cunard, which freed up

▼ *Mauretania was sent cruising before she was sold for scrap.* (Bill Miller Collection)

➤ *Farewell to the great Queen Mary. (Ian Boyle / Simplon Postcards)*

Did you know?
Names considered for *QE2* included William Shakespeare, British Queen, Winston Churchill and John F. Kennedy.

R.M.S. Queen Mary. Final Departure from Southampton, 1967. E1BG

much-needed capital for the shipping line. Despite this, the following year the company was forced to sell more ships in order to stay solvent.

On 8 May 1967, while at sea, the captains of *Queen Elizabeth* and *Queen Mary* simultaneously opened envelopes which contained details of their ships' retirements. *Queen Mary* departed first, sold to become a floating hotel in Long Beach, California. Her final Southampton departure, on 31 October 1967, began her longest peacetime voyage, which saw her round Cape Horn on her way to California.

Earlier that year, on 20 September, HM Queen Elizabeth II had launched Number 736. The new Cunarder, *Queen Elizabeth 2*, affectionately known as *QE2*, was moved to the fitting-out basin for completion.

In 1968, the Cunard Line retired four more ships. *Caronia* was withdrawn and sold to Star Shipping, being renamed *Columbia*. *Carinthia* and *Sylvania* were both withdrawn from service and sold to the Sitmar Line to be renamed *Fairsea* and *Fairwind*. After extensive refurbishments, these ships sailed successfully as cruise ships.

Queen Elizabeth was also retired from service in 1968. Early plans were made to convert the ship into a floating hotel at the burgeoning cruise hub of Fort Lauderdale. However, plans for her conversion fell through, resulting in her eventual sale to C.Y. Tung for use as a floating university in Hong Kong. Renamed *Seawise University*, the giant liner made her final voyage to Hong Kong, where conversion works began.

In Clydebank, Cunard eagerly awaited delivery of its new flagship. However, a series of malfunctions with the ship's boilers resulted in Cunard refusing to accept delivery of the ship until well into 1969.

QE2's maiden voyage departed Southampton on 30 May 1969. The debut of this new ship signalled Cunard's departure from the traditional. Exterior-wise, *QE2* was very modern, sporting a

Did you know?
QE2 was intended to be named Queen Elizabeth after her predecessor. HM Queen Elizabeth II personally altered the title to *Queen Elizabeth the Second*. Cunard opted to use the Arabic numeral '2' for its ship, and thus *QE2* was born.

single stylised mast and a funnel devoid of the traditional Cunard colours.

It was her interior, however, that would capture the most attention. Originally intended as a three-class liner, the decision was made to complete the ship as a two-class ship – first and tourist. On cruises she would operate with a single class.

◀ *Cunard's new flagship,*
Queen Elizabeth 2.
(Cunard Line)

Upon boarding *QE2*, passengers got their first very dramatic glimpse that this ship was no simple extension of the old Queens. Chrome, leather, aluminium, fibreglass and mood lighting were extensively used, resulting in a design with its roots firmly planted in the swinging '60s.

QE2 settled into a regular schedule of cruises and crossings. While the critics had questioned Cunard's wisdom in introducing a transatlantic liner in the age of the jet, *QE2* proved very popular, allowing Cunard

◄◄ *The 1960s' style of QE2's Double Down Room.* (Cunard Line)

◄ *The Look Out Bar aboard QE2 was very trendy.* (Cunard Line)

▲ *The QE2 was both a liner and a cruise ship.* (Cunard Line)

Did you know?

The first 'passenger' carried by *QE2* was HRH Prince Charles.

to repay £2.5 million of its Government loan by October 1969. *QE2* succeeded against the odds – in fact, so popular was the ship that in June 1970 she carried her 75,000th passenger, after just over one year of service.

On 8 January 1971, *QE2* rendered assistance to the liner *Antilles*. The French Line ship had struck a reef off the coast of Mustique in the Grenadines and was ablaze. *QE2* was able to rescue the ship's complement of 500 passengers and crew, which made headlines worldwide.

During 1971, a number of changes occurred at Cunard. The elder Cunarders, *Carmania* and *Franconia*, were retired from service. They were replaced by two new vessels, *Cunard Adventurer* in 1971 and *Cunard Ambassador* the following year.

Did you know?

Seawise University (ex-*Queen Elizabeth*) caught fire and burned out in Hong Kong Harbour before her conversion was completed. She was subsequently scrapped.

The year 1971 also saw Cunard sold to the Trafalgar House Company for £27.3 million. This ended 132 years of continual private ownership for Cunard Line; however, it provided much-needed capital for continued fleet revitalisation projects.

◄▲ *The Queens Room was QE2's first class lounge.* (Cunard Line)

▲ *The Columbia Restaurant aboard QE2 was for first class passengers.* (Cunard Line)

The acquisition of Cunard by Trafalgar House in 1971 provided an influx of capital for the line. *QE2* was treated to a £1 million refit, which involved prefabricated balcony suites being added to her top decks.

Cunard was also exploring cruising itineraries with its new ships, *Cunard Adventurer* and *Cunard Ambassador*. However, at just over 14,000 tons, the line found these ships too small and set about plans to replace them.

This desire to increase its cruising tonnage saw Cunard enter into an agreement with Overseas National Airways to purchase two 17,000-ton vessels which were under construction at the time. These ships entered service in 1976 and 1977, and were named *Cunard Countess* and *Cunard Princess* respectively. Pioneering itineraries in the Caribbean and Mediterranean, these popular cruise ships formed the backbone of Cunard's cruising expansion for the following two decades.

QE2 made headlines in 1972 when a bomb threat was received by the Cunard offices in New York. The crew conducted an extensive search aboard the ship, which

▼ QE2 *was given her first balcony accommodation after the Trafalgar House acquisition.* (Cunard Line)

voyages, accessing ports the old *Queens* had been unable to.

During the Falklands War of 1982, a number of Cunard ships were called into service. *QE2* was requisitioned for trooping

▼ *Aerial shot of the world's most iconic floating resort.* (Cunard Line)

was at sea en route to Southampton (via Cherbourg). A Royal Air Force Bomb Disposal Unit was parachuted into the sea and brought aboard *QE2* to conduct its own search, but nothing was found. The culprit was later caught for making similar threats to American Airlines, and was sentenced to twenty years in prison.

In 1974, *QE2* undertook her first world cruise, continuing the tradition inaugurated by *Laconia*. The design traits that allowed *QE2* to be successful as a cruise ship meant that she was able to easily undertake world

➤ *Margaret Thatcher aboard* QE2 *in honour of her service during the Falklands.* (Cunard Line)

Did you know?
The burnt-out hulk of *Queen Elizabeth* was used in the 1974 James Bond movie *The Man with the Golden Gun*.

duties and, after an extensive refit, sailed to the South Atlantic with 3,000 troops aboard.

Another Cunarder to participate in the conflict was the roll-on-roll-off vessel *Atlantic Conveyor*, as well as a fleet of helicopters, which was called up to provide supplies to the British Task Force. On 25 May 1982, she was hit by two Exocet missiles fired by a pair of Argentine Super Étendard jet fighters. The ship caught fire and was unable to be controlled, resulting in her being abandoned to burn out. Twelve crew, including her captain, died in the attack.

QE2 returned to Southampton from the Falklands campaign on 11 June 1982, where she was met by HM Queen Elizabeth, the Queen Mother, who was aboard the Royal Yacht *Britannia*. *QE2* was carrying survivors

Did you know?
Cunard Princess was originally to be named Cunard Conquest.

from the HMS *Antelope*, HMS *Coventry* and HMS *Ardent*. After disembarking her human cargo, *QE2* was given a lengthy refit and returned to Cunard service, painted for the first time with the traditional Cunard colours on her funnel.

After the cessation of hostilities in the Falklands, the *Cunard Countess* was chartered for six months from October 1982 by the British Government. She was used to transport troops between Ascension Island and Port Stanley whilst

the Falkland Islands airfield was being repaired.

During 1983, Trafalgar House acquired the Norwegian America Line, and with it their ships, *Sagafjord* and *Vistafjord*. These two magnificent liners were among the world's highest-rated vessels and commanded a fiercely loyal following. After briefly considering renaming the ships with traditional Cunard 'ia' names, it was decided to retain their Norwegian names and crew in order to secure the ongoing loyalty of their passengers.

The addition of *Sagafjord* and *Vistafjord* allowed Cunard to further diversify their cruising operation. This diversification was boosted in 1986 with the acquisition of the Sea Goddess brand. Sea Goddess had planned an ambitious project of creating a large fleet of luxury yachts; however, they failed financially after the completion of their second ship. With this acquisition, Cunard added *Sea Goddess I* and *Sea Goddess II* to its fleet. These ships, each with a passenger complement of just 100, were regarded at the time as 'the most luxurious ships ever to sail'.

In the years leading up to 1986, *QE2* had experienced worsening problems with her steam-propulsion system. After extensive research into the costs of building a new transatlantic liner, the decision was made to re-engine the beloved flagship.

Thus, in October 1986, the ship arrived in Bremerhaven, Germany, to be converted into a diesel-powered ship. This ended a tradition of continual steam crossings inaugurated by Cunard in 1840.

The refurbishment, which cost over $100 million, lasted until April 1987, and

◄◄ Cunard Countess *was Cunard's Caribbean cruise ship.* (Bill Miller Collection)

➤ *QE2's profile just prior to her 1986/87 refurbishment.* (Cunard Line)

Did you know?

Cunard marketed the Ritz Hotel on behalf of Trafalgar House.

was the largest marine conversion project undertaken at the time. Over 4,700 tons of scrap was removed from within *QE2* before being replaced by nine MAN B&W diesel electric engines. The funnel, which had been removed to facilitate easy access to the ship's engine room (via the funnel casing), was modified into a larger version of its already distinctive shape.

During the first Gulf War, *Cunard Princess* was chartered by the United States military as an Armed Forces Recreation Centre. The ship arrived in Bahrain on 24 December 1990 to take up this role. Initially it had been planned to operate the ship on three-day cruises around the Persian Gulf; however, for economic reasons she was instead moored in Bahrain. She re-entered normal service with Cunard on 19 October 1991.

The Cunard fleet was further increased in 1993 when the company entered into an agreement with the Crown Cruise Line. This venture resulted in Cunard operating Crown Cruise Line's three modern ships as *Cunard Crown Jewel*, *Cunard Crown Dynasty* and *Cunard Crown Monarch*, under the newly formed Cunard-Crown banner. *Cunard Countess* and *Cunard Princess* were marketed under the same four-star cruising guise, allowing the line to distinguish between the four- and five-star fleets.

Cunard Crown Monarch was sent to Australia to spearhead the line's attempt at challenging the long-held monopoly enjoyed by P&O's *Fairstar*. *Cunard Crown Monarch* was unsuccessful, and was withdrawn and sold in 1994.

Also in 1994, Cunard added yet another ship to its fleet when it purchased the Royal Viking Line and, with it, their flagship the *Royal Viking Sun*. *Royal Viking Sun* was considered one of the most luxurious

▲ QE2's *diesel engines.*
(Authors' Collection)

➤ Cunard Crown Monarch *was intended to capture the Australian market.* (Bill Miller Collection)

➤➤ QE2*'s rendezvous with the Royal Yacht Britannia.* (Cunard Line)

ships afloat, and was paired with *Sagafjord* and *Vistafjord*, and marketed under the Cunard-Royal Viking brand.

By late 1994, the post-jet age Cunard reached its peak in size within the cruise industry. The line was operating ten ships, as well as river boats and hotels that were owned by Trafalgar House. However, despite its size, Cunard's finances and market position were not healthy. Plagued with a mismatch of tonnage and with no new builds since *Cunard Princess*, the company was struggling to compete against the newer ships of Carnival Cruise Line, Royal Caribbean and Norwegian Cruise Line.

Trafalgar House took a number of actions in an attempt to ensure Cunard's survival. The most dramatic was a £45 million refurbishment of their flagship, *QE2*. The

refit was overseen by the British MET studio and completed at the Blohm & Voss shipyard in Hamburg. It aimed to recreate

QE2's interiors to extend her service life well into the twenty-first century.

To complete the refit, QE2 was taken out of service for one month, which proved to be too ambitious for the scale of the works. As a result, QE2 departed on her 1994 Christmas cruise incomplete. The wave of bad publicity following this decision resulted in significant public relations damage, not only to QE2 but also to the Cunard brand.

During 1995, Cunard divested themselves of *Cunard Princess* and *Cunard Crown Jewel* as they moved away from the mass cruising market and attempted to reorganise as a purely luxury brand.

In March 1996, the Trafalgar House Co. was sold to the Norwegian shipbuilding and engineering company Kværner for £904 million. The sale included Cunard Line. Kværner initially intended to sell Cunard on; however, after a lack of interest from within the industry, they placed Peter Ward at the head of the company and tasked him with the mission to return Cunard to profit.

To this end, the ageing *Sagafjord* was sold to Saga Cruises in 1996, following several incidents including a shipboard fire. Ward's tenure at Cunard was short-lived, with him resigning from the line in September 1996. He was replaced by his deputy Antti Pankakoski, who continued Kværner's plans to rationalise the Cunard business.

During 1997, the *Cunard Countess* and *Cunard Crown Dynasty* were withdrawn from service. The line would now concentrate only on the niche luxury cruise market. QE2's passenger complement was reduced to 1,500, allowing her to offer single-seating dining, a trait shared with the remainder of the fleet.

◀◀ QE2 *was always 'at home' in Sydney Harbour.* (Cunard Line)

Did you know?
Royal Viking Sun now sails with Holland America as *Prinsendam*.

➤ QE2 *in her post-1994 refit livery.* (Cunard Line)

➤➤ *HM The Queen aboard* QE2. (Cunard Line)

The five remaining ships of the Cunard fleet soldiered on, plagued by a lack of funds and unable to maintain the expected standards associated with a five-star luxury cruise brand. By 1998 it looked as if the Cunard name might finally fade away. With Kværner facing massive internal streamlining, it was only a matter of time before they divested themselves of the Cunard business, and it was feared that the Cunarders may be destined for the scrapyard.

Fortunately, in April 1998 the Carnival Corporation surprised the industry when it announced its acquisition of the Cunard Line. The purchase included all five of Cunard's ships.

During 1999, under the direction of Carnival's Larry Pimentel, the company was relaunched as Cunard Line Ltd. It included an internal merger with Carnival-owned Seabourn Cruise Line. *Royal Viking Sun* and the Sea Goddesses joined Seabourn to become *Seabourn Sun*, *Seabourn Goddess I* and *Seabourn Goddess II*.

QE2 and *Vistafjord* were given extensive refurbishments, the latter emerging as *Caronia*, and were placed under the Cunard banner, securing both their future and the future of the line they represented.

Millennium eve saw *QE2* and the newly renamed *Caronia* together off Barbados. Cunard was, for the first time in a decade, enjoying a synergy within its fleet. Both *QE2* and *Caronia* were positioned to attract cruise passengers seeking traditional British luxury. The ships shared the distinctive Cunard livery of matte black hull and white superstructure, making them both instantly identifiable as Cunarders.

The cruise industry was buzzing with the news that Cunard was planning a new ocean liner, code-named 'Project Queen

◄ *Resplendent in traditional Cunard livery, QE2 and* Caronia *shared millennium eve together.* (Cunard Line)

Mary'. This new build promised to create the longest, largest, widest and tallest ocean liner of all time. On 6 November 2000, a contract was signed with the French shipyard Chantiers de l'Atlantique to build this mammoth liner. The ship that was to become *Queen Mary 2* was given the yard number G-32.

Throughout the early years of the decade, *QE2* maintained a busy schedule of transatlantic crossings and cruises, while from 2001 *Caronia* undertook voyages out of British ports into Europe. The line regained its footing and settled into a comfortable position as Britain's most famous cruise brand. In fact, so confident was Carnival in Cunard that it allocated an 85,000-ton cruise ship for the line. To be constructed at Fincantieri, Porto Marghera, Italy, the ship – to be named

Queen Victoria – was due to Cunard in 2005.

In 2002, Cunard launched a strong marketing campaign as a precursor to *QM2*'s introduction into service. On 16 January 2002, Cunard's then president, Pamela Conover, inaugurated the steel-cutting process. By 1 December 2002, the ship was ready to be floated out and the fit-out process was started.

Cunard had a busy year in 2003. In their Miami office, the company was finalising the sale of *Caronia* to Saga Cruises. Saga, which owned *Caronia*'s sister ship *Saga Rose* (formerly *Sagafjord*), officially purchased *Caronia* on 30 May 2003. However, she remained in Cunard service until late 2004.

In France, *QM2*'s construction was continuing. By September 2003, her

◀◀ *The yet to be painted* QM2 *taking shape.* (Pam Massey)

Did you know?
QM2 was the first transatlantic ocean liner built since *QE2*.

Did you know?
QM2 was built at the same shipyard that created *Normandie*.

interior fit-out was nearing completion and in November she commenced her builder's sea trials. *QM2* achieved 29.62 knots, which successfully placed her as the second fastest passenger ship in service (after *QE2*'s 32.5 knots).

QM2 was officially accepted by Cunard on 22 December 2003. After a brief shakedown voyage (with only crew aboard), the ship, under the direction of Commodore R.W. Warwick, sailed into Southampton on Boxing Day as the world's largest passenger ship.

Cunard's newest Queen was named by HM Queen Elizabeth II on 8 January 2004, at a gala ceremony held in Southampton.

▼ QE2 *and* QM2 *in New York.* (Thad Constantine)

Her maiden voyage departed later that month. Despite her size and scale, she was not crowned flagship at the time of her introduction into service. That honour remained with *QE2* until April 2004, after the two Queens had completed their first tandem transatlantic crossing. A small ceremony was held aboard *QE2* to mark the occasion.

With the flagship status transferred to *QM2*, *QE2*'s role within the fleet changed. The veteran Cunarder would no longer be subjected to the rigours of regular transatlantic crossings, but instead would concentrate on European cruises.

In mid-2004, Cunard announced that *Queen Victoria*, currently under construction at Fincantieri, had been transferred to P&O Cruises (by now also part of the Carnival Corporation). A new *Queen Victoria* was commissioned on 3 December 2004, with design alterations taking into account factors that had made *QM2* a success. The new 90,000-ton Cunarder was also built at Fincantieri's Marghera shipyard, and her keel was laid on 12 May 2006.

With *Caronia*'s withdrawal from Cunard in late 2004, the fleet was reduced to just two ships. However, the fame of *QE2* plus the global interest in the new *QM2* meant that Cunard's name was never far from the headlines.

Throughout 2004, *QM2* made a number of historic maiden arrivals in European ports. One of the most memorable was her maiden call to Hamburg, where an estimated 1 million people lined the banks of the River Elbe to catch a glimpse of the ship.

◄◄ QM2 *is the only ship to have a planetarium.* (Authors' Collection)

Did you know?
QE2 has not yet been converted into a hotel and is now laid up in Dubai.

➤ *Accommodation aboard* Queen Victoria *is bright and modern.* (Authors' Collection)

Also in 2004, *QM2* was chartered for use as a hotel ship during the Athens Olympic Games. Docked in Piraeus, the ship played host to visiting presidents and prime ministers, as well as the US men's basketball team.

That same year, Cunard's headquarters were relocated to the Princess Cruises office (which had recently been acquired by Carnival Corporation) in Santa Clara, California. Throughout 2004 and 2005, the company merged many functions with Princess, and engaged in a Captain Exchange Programme which saw Princess and P&O captains take command of the Queens. The headquarters have since returned to the UK, with the company now operated out of Southampton's Carnival House.

In early 2007, the *QE2* and *QM2* made headlines again when they rendezvoused in Sydney Harbour. The event, which brought the city to a standstill, was the first time that two Cunard Queens had graced the iconic harbour since the Second World War.

On 15 January 2007, *Queen Victoria* was floated out, allowing the internal fit-out process to begin. Just prior to the float out, a bottle of Prosecco was broken against her side by Maureen Ryan, a Cunard Social Hostess, who had served on all four of the previous Cunard Queens.

The year 2007 also marked the fortieth anniversary of *QE2*'s launch. A number of special cruises were organised to mark this milestone. Voyages included a round-Britain cruise, where *QE2* returned to the River Clyde in September, coinciding with the month of her launch.

The celebrations took on a tone of sadness, however, due to the 18 June 2007

Did you know?
QM2, *Queen Victoria* and *Queen Elizabeth* are all bigger (by tonnage) than the original Queens.

◄◄ Queen Victoria *in Sydney, on her maiden call to the Australian city.* (Peter F. Williams)

◄ QE2 *and* Queen Victoria *rendezvous in Sydney.* (Cunard Line)

announcement that *QE2* was to be retired from Cunard service. She had been sold to Istithmar, the investment arm of Dubai World, for £50.5 million, with the intention to use her as a floating hotel at the Palm Jumeirah in Dubai.

Did you know?
HM Queen Elizabeth II was present at the launch of all three Elizabeths.

This sadness notwithstanding, *QE2* enjoyed a jubilant farewell season. *Queen Victoria* had entered Cunard service in December 2007 and, during the start of her world cruise in January the following year, she undertook a tandem crossing

'Dubai is a maritime nation and we understand the rich heritage of *QE2*. She is coming to a home where she will be cherished.'

Dubai World Chairman,
Sultan Ahmed bin Sulayem.

with *QE2* before meeting *QM2* in New York.

QE2's farewell season involved a number of meetings with her fleet mates. She rendezvoused with *Queen Victoria* in Fort Lauderdale and Sydney during their 2008 world cruises, and met both ships in Southampton during April 2008. She bid farewell to *Queen Victoria* in Zeebrugge and *QM2* in Southampton, before finally departing on her last voyage to Dubai on 11 November 2008, under the command of Captain Ian McNaught.

Captain Ian McNaught recalls leaving his beloved *QE2* for the final time:

Years before, one of my predecessors told me, 'You look after her and she will look after you'. With that in mind, as I stood at the top of the gangway in five deck forward, I just touched the hull and said thank you, and then went down the gangway, climbed into the taxi and went off without looking back.

With *QE2*'s withdrawal from service on 27 November, Cunard was once again a two-ship fleet. This situation wasn't to last, however, as the company had ordered a sister ship for *Queen Victoria* in October 2007.

At 90,400 tons, this ship was named *Queen Elizabeth*. She set off on her maiden

Did you know?
During the Carnival years, Cunard's headquarters have been in Miami (Florida) and Santa Clara (California). They have now returned to Southampton.

associated with the two previous Elizabeths, taking most of its inspiration from the Art Deco style of her 1940s' namesake.

With the *Queen Elizabeth* delivered, Cunard once again had a three-ship fleet. The line set about creating a series of unique events to celebrate the new ship's arrival; including a tandem transatlantic crossing with *Queen Victoria* in January 2011 followed by a three ship rendezvous in New York harbour.

During HM Queen Elizabeth II's Diamond Jubilee, the three Cunarders met in Southampton. *QM2* carried a large banner stating 'Congratulations Ma'am' and the three vessels sounded their whistles in honour of the Queen.

In response to her popularity in Australia and New Zealand, since 2013 Cunard have sent their flagship *QM2* on extended voyages

voyage on 12 October 2010, after being named by HM Queen Elizabeth II in Southampton. *Queen Elizabeth*'s interior was designed to reflect the nostalgia

in the region. This was continued in 2015 with *QM2* and *Queen Victoria* rendezvousing in Sydney in March. *QM2* then sailed on a 'round New Zealand' cruise, before returning to Australian waters.

To celebrate the 175th anniversary, Cunard arranged a number of special voyages in 2015. In May, *Queen Victoria* paid tribute to the *Lusitania* on a special 100th anniversary sailing calling at Cork (formerly Queenstown), near by where the *Lusitania* sunk.

Also in 2015, a ceremonial 'meeting of the Queens' in Liverpool saw Cunard return to its birthplace. The iconic Cunard Building remains a dominant presence in Liverpool, forming part of the city's 'Three Graces'. On 4 July 2015, *QM2*'s departure from Liverpool bound for Boston retraced the voyage taken by Britannia exactly 175 years earlier.

For 175 years, Cunard has endured and thrived. Despite wars, changing economies, the advance of the jet and periods of mismanagement, the solid foundations set by its founder, Sir Samuel Cunard has seen the line flourish.

Cunard Line is a reminder to us all, of the inspiring leadership shown by that early pioneer. Long may Cunard prosper!

▼ *The three Queens, Elizabeth, Victoria and Mary 2, in 2011.* (Cunard Line)

BIBLIOGRAPHY

Bacon, E.M., *Manual of Ship Subsidies*, Project Gutenberg, e-Book (1911)

Braynard, F.O. and Miller, W.H., *Picture History of the Cunard Line*, Dover, United Kingdom (1991)

Chirnside, M., Aquitania: *The Ship Beautiful*, The History Press, United Kingdom (2009)

Cowell, A., 'Belfast Shipyard Loses Bid to Build *Queen Mary 2*, and Many Jobs', *New York Times*, 11 March 2000

De Kerbrech, R., *Ships of the White Star Line*, Ian Allen Publishing, United Kingdom (2009)

Frame, C. and Cross, R., *The* QE2 *Story*, The History Press, United Kingdom (2009)

Gandy, M., 'The Britannia Cup', *The Antiques Magazine*, July 1982 ed. Volume 122, pp.156–8 (1982)

Granger Blair, W., 'B.O.A.C. buys out Cunard's share; $32.2-Million price to help ship line offset losses', *New York Times*, 16 September 1966, p.55 (1966)

Grant, R.G., *Flight: The Complete History*, Dorling Kindersley Ltd, United Kingdom (2007)

Harding, S., *Gray Ghost: The RMS* Queen Mary *at War*, Pictorial Histories Publishing Co., United States of America (1982)

Hutchings, D.F., *RMS* Queen Elizabeth – *From Victory to Valhalla*, Kingfisher Publications, United Kingdom (1990)

Ipsen, E., 'Kværner is Close to Bidding for Troubled Group: Lifeline for Trafalgar House?', *New York Times*, 28 February 1996

Jones, S., '*QE2* sold to become Floating Hotel', *Travel Weekly*, 18 June 2007

Langley, J.G., *Steam Lion: A Biography of Samuel Cunard*, Brick Tower Press, United States of America (2006)

Maxtone-Graham, J. and Lloyd, H., Queen Mary 2: *The Greatest Ocean Liner of Our Time*, Bulfinch, United Kingdom (2004)

McCutcheon, J., *Cunard: A Photographic History*, Tempus, United Kingdom (2004)

McDowell, E., 'Chief's Strategy for Ailing Cruise Line', *New York Times*, 6 August 1996

Miller, W.H., *SS* United States: *Speed Queen of the Seas*, Amberley, United Kingdom (2010)

Miller, W.H., *Picture History of the* Queen Mary *and* Queen
    Elizabeth, Dover, United Kingdom (2001)
Miller, W.H., *Picture History of British Ocean Liners: 1900 to the
    Present*, Dover, United Kingdom (2001)
Miller, W.H., *Pictorial Encyclopaedia of Ocean Liners 1860–1994*,
    Dover, United Kingdom (1995)
Osborne, B.D. and Armstrong, R., *Scotland's Greatest Ships*,
    Luthan Press Ltd, United Kingdom (2007)
Plisson, P., Queen Mary 2*: The Birth of a Legend*, Harry N.
    Abrams, United Kingdom (2004)
Unknown, 'Cunard Chief Resigns', *Herald Scotland*, 21 Sep 1996.
Williams, D., *Cunard's Legendary Queens of the Seas*, Ian Allen
    Publishing, United Kingdom (2004)
Wills, E., *The Fleet 1840–2004: Cunard's Flagships and Floating
    Palaces from the Earliest Days of Steam to* Queen Mary 2,
    Open Agency, United Kingdom (2004)

Cunard Line (2009) Onboard Promotional Material (various versions)
Cunard Line (2009) *Queen Mary 2*: Technical and Bridge Facts
    (various versions)

FILM:

Queen Mary Launch, *c.*1934

Queen Elizabeth Launch, *c.*1938

PERSONAL CONVERSATIONS:

Commodore R.W. Warwick

Captain Ian McNaught

John Langley, Cunard Steamship Society

Caroline Matheson, Cunard Insights

Cunard Line PR Executive M. Gallagher

WEBSITES:

Chris' Cunard Page: http://www.chriscunard.com/

Cunard's Official Website:http://www.cunard.com/

Rob Lightbody's *QE2* Website: http://www.roblightbody.com/
liners/qe-2/qe230.htm

A multimedia history of the First World War:

http://www.firstworldwar.com/source/bryanlusitaniaprotest.htm

FOR FURTHER READING, AVAILABLE FROM THE HISTORY PRESS:

If you are interested in more information and photographs of *QM2*:
QM2: *A Photographic Journey*, Chris Frame and Rachelle Cross.
The QM2 *Story*, Chris Frame and Rachelle Cross.

If you are interested in more information and photographs of *QE2*:
QE2: *A Photographic Journey*, Chris Frame and Rachelle Cross.
The QE2 *Story*, Chris Frame and Rachelle Cross.

If you are interested in more information and photographs of *Queen Victoria*:
Queen Victoria: *A Photographic Journey*, Chris Frame and Rachelle Cross.

If you are interested in more information and photographs of *Queen Elizabeth* (2010):
Queen Elizabeth: *A Photographic Journey*, Chris Frame and Rachelle Cross.

Photographic Notice:
Photographic copyright remains with the collection owner/photographer acknowledged next to each image within this book. All images used within this book were done so with the express permission of the collection owner/photographer.